The Moon Lady and Her Festival

by Libby McCord

illustrated by CD Hullinger

PEARSON

Scott
Foresman

Editorial Offices: Glenview, Illinois • Parsippany, New Jersey • New York, New York
Sales Offices: Needham, Massachusetts • Duluth, Georgia • Glenview, Illinois
Coppell, Texas • Ontario, California • Mesa, Arizona

Long ago, in China, there was a man
named Yi. Yi was a great archer. He
had a beautiful wife named Chang-O.
Yi and Chang-O loved each other very
much.

One day, ten suns shone and the
earth became very dry. So the ruler
asked Yi to shoot down nine of the suns.

Yi knocked all but one sun out of the sky. That sun shines on Earth today.

As thanks, Yi got a magic pill. It would let him live forever! But, first, he had to pray for a year to get ready for the magic. Yi hid the pill in his house.

When Chang-O was home alone, she smelled a delightful smell. She followed her nose. Then she saw a beam of light coming through a crack.

It was the magic pill. Chang-O ate it to see what would happen.

Just then, Yi came home. He saw Chang-O floating out the window.

"No!" Yi cried. "Do not go away!"

"I was wrong, but I cannot stop!" she called back.

Chang-O flew up into the night sky.
Yi chased her as far as he could. But the
winds blew him back to Earth.

Chang-O flew straight up to the
moon! She shivered. The moon was a
cold, silent place, full of dusty rocks.

Chang-O met a rabbit under a tree.

"Hello," said Chang-O. "Is it always cold here?"

"Always," the rabbit said.

"Do you know how to make me a special drink so I can go back to Earth?" asked Chang-O.

The rabbit tried, but he could not make the right drink. So Chang-O could not fly. She had to stay there forever. She became goddess of the moon.

Yi became the god of the sun and lived in the Palace of the Sun.

Yi was allowed to visit Chang-O on the night of the full moon every month.

Yi and Chang-O built the Palace of Great Cold. The outside walls were silver. Inside, the rooms were the colors of the rainbow.

After their day together the two had to part.

"Good-bye!" Chang-O waved.

"Good-bye!" called Yi. He flew back to the sun.

They longed for each other—until the next full moon.

Chinese people look up at the full moon and still think of this story. Every year, they tell it to their children during the Moon Festival.

The Moon Festival also celebrates the end of harvest. People give thanks for what they have.

People celebrate the Moon Festival in many ways. They make pictures of the moon goddess. They put on puppet shows about Chang-O and Yi. Children like Chang-O because they think she knows about their secret wishes.

At the Moon Festival, people put out
bowls of water to reflect the moon. They
light candles and read moon poems.
People also have foods that are
symbols of the moon. They have round
fruit, like grapes, peaches, and melons.

People eat moon cakes with a boiled egg in the middle. Some cakes have a picture of the moon rabbit on top.

Families get together and have fun. They tell stories about the moon. Then they eat lots of moon cakes!

The Moon Festival

The Moon Festival is very important in China. You have read one Moon Festival story. There are many other stories as well. One story is about moon cakes.

A long time ago the Chinese were under the rule of the Mongols. The Mongols were cruel to the Chinese. The Chinese decided to fight against them. During one Moon Festival, the Chinese bakers hid messages in the moon cakes. The messages told people when to fight the Mongols.

The start of the fighting suprised the Mongols. The Chinese won, so they were no longer ruled by the Mongols.

This story is one reason that moon cakes are important to Chinese culture.